Great ideas—for a great need! *A Little Book of Romance* is packed with powerful and playful ways to keep the passion in your marriage!

Pam and Bill Farrell, authors
Men Are Like Waffles, Women Are Like Spaghetti

A Little Book of Romance will thrill your heart, put your romance into high gear, and create vibrations of love. Every married person should have this fabulous book on the coffee table to refer to constantly, and every single person should keep it handy for the future. You will love this book!

Kathy Collard Miller, speaker and author
Princess to Princess

Here's proof that marital love isn't monotonous. This book is packed with inspiration for intimacy, sizzle for sex, and poetry for passion.

Deb Strubel
BigScore Productions

When we are first married, romance comes naturally. However as the years go by and life gets in the way, loving our mate extravagantly becomes passé. I am glad to have contributed to this clever collection of ideas and inspiration to bring spice and surprise back to marriage.

Marita Littauer, speaker, author,
and president of CLASServices Inc.

Not since Marabel Morgan's mega-bestseller, *Total Woman*, has a book come along that ignites the fires of romance. Debra White Smith has written a masterpiece on love at its best. This book is guaranteed to rekindle the fires of romance in many homes.

Stan Toler, author
Minute Motivator series

a little book of
Romance

Debra White Smith

Congratulations Rachel!

Love,
Melanie "

HARVEST HOUSE PUBLISHERS

EUGENE, OREGON

Unless otherwise indicated, Scripture quotations are taken from the HOLY BIBLE, NEW INTERNATIONAL VERSION®. NIV®. Copyright © 1973, 1978, 1984 by the International Bible Society. Used by permission of Zondervan Publishing House. The "NIV" and "New International Version" trademarks are registered in the United States Patent and Trademark Office by International Bible Society.

Published in association with the literary agency of Alive Communications, Inc., 7680 Goddard Street, Ste. #200, Colorado Springs, CO 80920.

Every effort has been made to give proper credit for all stories, poems, and quotations. If for any reason proper credit has not been given, please notify the author or publisher and proper notation will be given on future printing.

Cover by Garborg Design Works, Savage, Minnesota

A LITTLE BOOK OF ROMANCE
Formerly *101 Ways to Romance Your Marriage*
Copyright © 2003 by Debra White Smith
Published 2003/2008 by Harvest House Publishers
Eugene, Oregon 97402
www. harvesthousepublishers.com

Library of Congress Cataloging-in-Publication Data

Smith, Debra White.
  [101 ways to romance your marriage]
  A little book of romance / Debra White Smith.
     p. cm.
  Originally published: 101 ways to romance your marriage. Eugene, OR.: Harvest House Publishers, ©2003.
  ISBN 13: 978-0-7369-2130-5
  ISBN 10: 0-7369-2130-3
  1. Marriage—Psychological aspects. 2. Love. 3. Sexual excitement.
  4. Man-woman relationships—Miscellanea. I. Title.

HQ734.S713 2008
248.8'44—dc21

                                                        2008016374

Printed in the United States of America

08 09 10 11 12 13 14 / BP-NI / 7 6 5 4 3 2 1

Contents

· · · · · · · · · · ·

BE IMAGINATIVE AND BOLD!

Deep in the heart of most men and women is the desire for a loving, romantic relationship—that's what dreams are made of. This is why so many movies include a romantic element. Sometimes even in the roughest, toughest he-man adventure there will be a romantic thread that affects the hearts of male and female viewers.

Gender influences how we interpret romance. Women are more inclined to the warm, tender side of romance while men have a tendency to think of the physical side. That's why we've divided this book into sections: one for men, one for women, and one for both of you. The suggestions in this book will give you plenty of ideas to please your mate. Some of them are fun things my husband and I have done for each other. Others are from couples who have successful marriages and enjoy keeping their love active and alive.

After 25 years of marriage, my husband and I have a dynamic marriage that many people wish they had. We've learned the best marriages happen when both spouses invest time in keeping the relationship fresh and healthy. And the most exhilarating marriages happen when both people get creative and maybe even a little daring.

So be bold and try something new. Experiment. Be imaginative and resourceful. Romance can happen regardless of budget, kids, or circumstances. Take the time to "Wow!" your partner. Maybe you'll even dream up a new angle on an old trick that will dazzle you both.

Have fun!

Debra White Smith

101 WAYS

I need 101 ways to
confront monotony,
enrich monogamy,
fulfill passion,
renew vitality.

Lord,
show me where I can discover
the surprising,
the spontaneous,
the excitement,
the spark.

I long for 101 ways to
a blazing love affair,
a match made in heaven,
a dream come true,
a key to bliss.

I seek 101 ways to
romance my marriage,
unleash desire,
express true love,
revive our fire.

R.N. HAWKINS & DEBRA WHITE SMITH

PART ONE

Making Your Hero Sizzle

A good man is hard to find.
Once you find him,
do everything in your power
to make him happy.

One way a wife loves her husband is to see him as her hero. Allowing her husband to *be* her hero when danger lurks is easy for many women. But husbands need to feel like heroes every day.

Most men yearn to be needed—*really needed*. Many of the tasks husbands offer assistance on can be handled by wives, so wives say, "Oh, don't get up. I'll take care of it." But I encourage you to gladly accept your guy's assistance and thank him for helping. I'm not advocating pretending weakness or stupidity, but give your man opportunities to rescue you, to use his masculine strength for you.

I wonder if our female ancestors understood the male temperament well when they "accidentally" dropped a handkerchief. The next time you have the chance, try "dropping your own handkerchief" and throw in a saucy wink to round things off.

MY HERO

When we moved into our unfinished home, I never considered the un-sealed crevices until one night I heard fluttering...

I open my eyes. In the dim moonlight pouring through the windows I see a small, dark object swooping over our bed. *A bat!*

Letting out a squeal, I dive under the sheet and give my husband a sharp jab. "Wake up!" Jab. "There's a bat in here!"

"Huh? Oh. Whoa!"

There's a sudden thrashing of arms and legs. "Don't lift the sheet!" I squeak.

My husband's dark, handsome head pokes under my fabric sanctuary. "What?"

"I said, 'Don't lift the sheet!' And close the door! I don't want it getting into the kids' rooms."

"You stay here, honey. I'll take care of it." My strong ex-Marine carefully slithers out from under the sheet.

I pull the covering more closely about me,

forming a tiny slit for my eyes so I can watch.

Clad in jockey shorts, my hero crawls to the door, pushes it shut, and heads to the closet. He emerges with a tennis racket.

Flutter, flutter, swoop...

The bat heads straight for him. My husband stands up and slashes wildly with the tennis racquet. Swish! Swish! Swish!

"You missed! Turn on the light!"

"Can't. He'll take cover."

Flutter, flutter...

Swish! Crack!

I eye the gouge in our new bed. "Aim the other way!"

Flutter, flutter, swoop...

Swish! Smack!

A small black object hurls past my head and onto my pillow. I dive under the sheet.

I feel a gentle pat on my covered head. "You can come out now, hon. It's dead."

I look at the broken black thing on his racquet and shudder. Giving me a grin that makes me tingle, my hero swaggers to the bathroom to dispose of his vanquished foe.

—Dorothy Clark

*R*ecreate your honeymoon night. Send your husband a special wedding-type invitation announcing that you are taking him on a second honeymoon. If you can't go back to the same place where you stayed, decorate your bedroom in themes from your honeymoon or stay in a similar place. Put on your wedding gown or buy something lacy to wear. Underneath the gown, wear lingerie like what you wore that first night. Find recordings of songs from your wedding and play them in the bedroom or hotel room. On the night of the big event, wait for your husband in the bedroom, and ask him to help you take off your wedding dress.

Shop for sexy lingerie as often as you can afford it. You will be surprised at how much anticipation you develop as you think about modeling the new piece for your husband and imagine his response. Most guys accept the fact that their wives aren't model perfect because most guys aren't perfect themselves. When you realize your body isn't an issue, you become free to romance your husband with abandon!

Roll a red rose inside your husband's daily newspaper or favorite magazine. Deliver it with a juicy, hot kiss and his favorite beverage.

∘ ∘ ∘

Watch the sunrise or sunset together.

AMBER MILLER

∘ ∘ ∘

On our tenth wedding anniversary, I sent a care package to my husband's job. When he opened it, he found a note that said, "Read Song of Solomon 7:11." ("Come, my lover, let us go to the countryside, let us spend the night in the villages.") I also included a small bottle of massage oil and some scented soap—and the brochure for the cabin I'd rented for the night. He was quite surprised when he put the "puzzle" together, and I felt very sneaky!

—CHRISTIE HAGERMAN

*A*bsence really does make the heart grow fonder. My husband works hard every day, and then he comes home to the chaos of a busy household with kids and a dog. Sometimes he feels overwhelmed. When it seems as though we need a little spark, I send him away—to visit relatives, to go skiing, to spend some quiet time in the mountains. At first he loves the peace and quiet, but after about a day and a half, he always comes rushing home, filled with love and usually bearing flowers.

—MINDY STARNS CLARK

To My Dear and Loving Husband

If ever two were one then surely we.
If ever man were loved by wife, then thee;
If ever wife were happy in a man,
Compare with me, ye women, if you can.
I prize thy love more than whole mines of gold
Or the riches that the East doth hold.
My love is such that rivers cannot quench,
Nor aught but love from thee give recompense.
Thy love is such I can no way repay,
The heavens reward thee manifold, I pray.
Then while we live, in love let's so persevere
That when we live no more, we may live ever.

ANNE BRADSTREET (1612–1672)

*C*all your man at work and read a pas-
sage from Song of Songs such as 2:8-9
and 2:16-17:

> *Listen! My Lover!*
> *Look! Here he comes*
> *leaping across the mountains,*
> *bounding over the hills.*
> *My lover is like a gazelle or a young stag.*
> *Look! There he stands behind our wall,*
> *gazing through the lattice....*

Song of Songs 2:8-9

> *My lover is mine and I am his;*
> *he browses among the lilies*
> *Until the day breaks and the shadows flee,*
> *turn, my lover, and be like a gazelle*
> *or like a young stag on the rugged hills.*

Song of Songs 2:16-17

*F*ind out what your husband's favorite fashion from the past is, such as in the 50s, 60s, 70s—or even the 1800s. Declare a night alone at home "A Visit to the Past." Play music from his favorite era. Dress in that style. If possible, prepare a meal from that time. Tell him you're his "date from the past," and let your imagination run wild!

Record a personal greeting on a CD for your husband to play in his vehicle's stereo. Put a sticky note on the disc that reads "Play Me." When your husband plays the recording he will be greeted by you—his lover. You can make the recording as cute and sassy as you like or as sensual as you dare.

I keep all my "romancing" paraphernalia in a bedside drawer. I store candles, matches, scented lotions, and flavored lip glosses. I'm much more apt to use these items and make our time more special if things are conveniently at hand.

—ROSANNA HORST

*B*e innovative with simple things. Recently I purchased a mug for my husband. Before I gift wrapped it, I placed sexy underwear along with a note inside the mug. It created an air of anticipation of what was to come. I got a charge out of watching his reaction.

—CINDY NORMAN

INTRODUCTIONS

Somebody once told me when making intro-
ductions to remember this subtle difference.
When introducing my husband to others I say,
"This is Paul, my husband," rather than
"this is my husband, Paul."
The first recognizes that Paul is a unique, in-
dependent person who chose me to marry.
The latter sounds as if his identity is in me.
I want to remember that he chose
me. It puts a twinkle in my heart.

BRENDA NIXON

*F*ill a big box with tissue paper and place three items inside—a note, your husband's favorite romantic CD, and a small box (a heart-shaped box with a lid is good, but any small box will do). On the note write, "Tonight I've made plans for us. Bring the CD and wear what's in the box." When he opens the box, he'll find it's empty. You take it from there!

—KATHLEEN Y'BARBO

The first Easter my husband and I were married I hid treasure-hunt notes all around the house with candy and little gifts such as a picture frame with a picture of us.

I set the alarm to wake him up early Easter morning. I got up a few minutes before he did and hid in the closet. When the alarm went off he found an Easter basket with a plastic egg next to him. Inside was a hint to the next location.

As he moved through the house following clues, I was in the bedroom setting up candles and the final hint. When the second to last hint led him into our room, there were candles lit throughout the room and a giant Hershey's kiss with little kisses in the shape of a heart in the middle of the bed. One more plastic egg note told him to close his eyes and wait. I came out of the bathroom wearing the nightie he liked best.

We'll never forget that Easter egg hunt!

—CRYSTAL OLSON

I prepared dinner for the kids ahead of time. After their dinner they became engrossed in a movie. When my husband walked through the door I pulled him into the bedroom and locked the door. I had dinner set for two on a small table. I proceeded to undress him to his boxers and then lovingly massaged his back with oil until he was completely relaxed. Next, I fed him dinner. After dinner, I asked for a massage.

—BETH GODDARD

Break the pattern of ordinary in your life. Adventure and romance wait a few feet outside the circle in which you exist. Step outside and explore the possibilities. You'll never know what you'll discover unless you try.

AMBER MILLER

A friend wanted to surprise her hus-band, who loved Oriental themes. She decided to have him find her dressed as a geisha at a hotel. Another friend and I began working on a kimono. The three of us met at my house to measure, cut, and sew for several weeks. Research into the world of the geisha proved to be interesting for all of us. We learned what hairstyles and make-up applications we should use.

The day finally arrived. My friend invited her husband to meet her for lunch at a local restaurant. After eating, she left the table on the pretext of using the restroom, paid the bill, and slipped an envelope to the waitress asking that it be given to her husband. The message instructed him to go to a local spa for a prepaid massage.

From there she created a scavenger hunt for him. He found notes in various places and had to pick up chocolates, snacks, his camera, and some clothes. The final clue gave directions to a bed-and-breakfast.

Meanwhile, we were hard at work. We got to the inn and transformed our friend into a dark-coifed geisha, complete with homemade kimono, wig, and makeup.

The moment my friend's husband opened the door was priceless. My friend and I dragged him into the room, caught a glimpse of his stunned face, and quickly escaped amid giggles and laughter.

This would be easy to do at home as well. Transform your bedroom or any other room in the house for an evening. Sheets could be used to cover the furniture. Netting and sheer fabrics are inexpensive as well. Pillows, some theme music, and a few candles will set the mood. There is no limit! Try an Arabian Nights theme with you belly dancing. Or have a picnic outside under the stars…or under stars made with lights and sheets on the ceiling. It takes some preplanning, but it's worth the effort to surprise your mate with something fun!

—ALLISON WILSON

*L*et your husband know he is one-of-a-kind to you. Tell him he stands apart in your eyes. Speak intimately of his body. Describe to your husband his hair, eyes, cheeks, lips, arms, legs, and mouth—all his physical attributes. Show him you find him attractive.

—PHILIP ATTEBERY

∘ ∘ ∘

Free yourself. Change your pattern.
Jolt the old, familiar things into new,
unfamiliar things. Be the first to
make the effort to change, and
your spouse is sure to follow.

AMBER MILLER

∘ ∘ ∘

Create a festive holiday room. If you have a canopy bed, decorate it around the top with appropriate items, such as garlands and mini-lights for Christmas. Or secure the decorations to the ceiling or upper edge of the walls. Buy a generous supply of scented candles and place them about. Play an instrumental CD softly. Purchase a special gift for your hubby. For Christmas, shop the lingerie department for a sexy "Mrs. Claus" look. Cut both side seams of a red nightie and apply self-adhesive Velcro strips up and down both sides. You now have a pull-away Mrs. Santa suit!

Arrange for the kids to be away for the night. Order dinner in or prepare a special meal in advance. Light the candles and turn on the music and the twinkle lights. Enjoy your meal and then encourage your husband to prepare for bed in the wonderland that is your bedroom. Sneak into the bathroom, put on your lingerie, and surprise him!

—CJ AND LYNETTE SOWELL

The next time you or your husband go out of town, make him anticipate when you're back together. Buy a small photo album with pockets. Cut paper to fit inside the pockets so the surprises you insert can't be seen. Label each one in countdown format. Some surprise ideas are:

- a picture of the two of you together
- a coupon for dinner or something sexy
- a toothpick with "I'd pick you again"
- a coupon for a massage
- a packet of sugar with "You're so sweet"
- two movie tickets
- a paper clip with "You hold me together"
- a rubber band with "Bound by love"
- a poem written from your heart
- hot chocolate mix with "I'm hot for you"

—CHRISTY BARRITT

*H*ave some glamor shots taken especially for your husband. Many studios offer tasteful yet sexy poses that your husband will find appealing. One of the sexiest shots I've ever seen was of a woman who put on her husband's dress shirt and hat with no slacks. She was well covered, yet the photo spoke of marital intimacy.

Your Kiss

Your kiss lingers.
*Our first kiss went beyond
my lips into my heart.
There it lingers:
ever sweet, always moist,
promising, disturbing, exciting.*

Your kiss captured me.
*Your lips created a blaze
of ecstasy within my being.
There it burns ever strong,
always hot, blazing, arousing, fulfilling.*

R.N. Hawkins

Many men enjoy receiving a tasteful, public display of admiration. My husband loved these ideas.

1. When I knew his coworkers were bringing him home, I hung "welcome home" balloons on the mailbox.

2. I went to the parking lot of his office and covered his car window with notes that had phrases I knew wouldn't embarrass him but would make him feel loved, such as "I love you" and "You're awesome!"

3. I wrote on the bathroom mirror with lipstick, "I love you, James!" and then pressed my lips to the mirror to make a few kisses. (I knew he would like it, but I was surprised that he left it there all week for our visitors to see.)

—K. JACKSON

*D*oes your husband carry a pager? Together come up with a number sequence
that means "I love you"—and page him often. My husband and I use the message "1 4
3," which means "I love you" to us. We feel
connected as we think of each other.

—KATHY COLLARD MILLER

*M*y husband often enjoys relaxing in a hot bath, especially after a long stressful day at work. So after dinner surprise your guy with a hot bath ready and waiting for him. You can get his attention after he's relaxing by joining him. Or, if your husband doesn't like hot baths, surprise him by stepping into the shower with him.

—BETH GODDARD

ROMANTIC GRACE

If your husband isn't the most romantic man
on the planet, give him some grace. Start
seriously romancing him, showing him what
romance is. It might take a while for him to
catch on, but be patient and enjoy the process!

After I'd been romancing my husband
for about a year, he looked at me
and said, "I don't know if I even
know how to be romantic."

Shortly after that, he hired a
quartet to serenade me in a restaurant.

I believe a lot of men want to be more
romantic than they are. So have an
understanding attitude and be romantic!

Solomon says that his lover is a garden. She responds by inviting him to "come into his garden and taste its choice fruits" (Song of Songs 4:16). Do you ever initiate physical intimacy with your husband? He might want you to! Talk about your love for him and everything about him, and then lead him into the bliss of physical intimacy.

—PHILIP ATTEBERY

One evening I knew my husband was going to be home late. I lit candles around the bedroom and put on a lacy, white nightie. I arranged the pillows so that I could lie in the middle of the bed and fluffed my lingerie around me. I heard him suck in his breath when he walked into the room. I took his breath away!

—BETH GODDARD

Buy your husband a superhero T-shirt and write him a note telling him why he is your personal hero.

—CHER ANDERSON

∘ ∘ ∘

Don't rely on prepackaged romance to solve your problems. Relish the everyday things that can add romance…a walk on a beach, hand-in-hand, at midnight. Enjoy the gifts of life that are free. Don't spend all your time striving for what's not free, and then make yourself too exhausted to enjoy it.

AMBER MILLER

∘ ∘ ∘

*A*fter a particularly amorous evening together, use your husband's bathroom mirror as a messenger of love. Take a red lipstick and write, "Wow!" in big letters on the mirror. He'll get the point and enjoy a sexy chuckle.

I recently asked my husband what his fantasy was. You should have seen the look on his face. His jaw dropped and he asked "Are you serious? Do you really want to know?" I wondered, *Haven't I ever asked him what he wants?* The answer was a resounding, "No!" I simply assumed something or tried to figure it out on my own. Asking him that question opened up an entirely new level of communication between us.

Find a way to sneak the question into your husband's day. Maybe leave a card just for him. Or send him a package at work. Make sure to mark the box "private," and place some sexy lingerie inside with a note: "What is your fantasy? Tell me. I want to fulfill it!"

—BETH GODDARD

My husband and I are avid outdoors people, and we love to hunt and fish in the fall. In order to prepare for hunting season, we start going to our leased acres several months before deer season begins. During one of these visits to the woods, I secretly packed a picnic lunch. I then set it out in the box stand while my husband put out the corn for the deer. The next time he climbed into the deer stand, he was pleasantly surprised and felt very special. We were able to commune with nature and with each other. He loved it.

—KIMBERLY OWENS

I had flowers sent to my husband's office with a card that said "Happy anniversary! Hurry home!"

I shopped for the ingredients to make a lovely dinner. I got home, did the dinner prep work, and put it all aside. I went into the bedroom and found something small and black hanging on our four poster bed with an anniversary card. (He hadn't forgotten after all.) I relaxed in a bubble bath and put my present on. I lit candles in the bedroom and put something bubbly in the silver bucket next to the bed with two crystal flutes. It was nearly time for him to get home. I sat on the bed and read my romance novel. I waited.

The dogs barked, and I heard his car door. I tucked the romance novel away and placed myself artfully across the bed. He was so excited to see me! The night left me breathless and thrilled my husband!

—MARITA LITTAUER

Most husbands have hobbies like fishing, golfing, or hunting. You can take his hobby and create a special time of friendship, bonding, and even romance.

One afternoon I suggested we go fishing. My husband was surprised! When we first began dating he asked if I could bait a hook. My ready reply was, "Yes." But we never went fishing after we got married. My reason was, "Well, just because I *can* bait a hook, doesn't meant I *want* to bait a hook."

This time I took the initiative to do something he loves with him. We went to his favorite fishing spot. I took great interest in everything he said. The day turned out to be a relaxing time for both of us, bringing us even closer. Few things "wow" a man more than a wife who takes an interest in and is willing to be a part of his hobby.

—BETH GODDARD

*L*eave a note for your husband when he gets home from work. The note might say something like, "I'm a secret admirer of yours, please meet me at _____ (a special restaurant of your choice) at 7:00 PM. I'll be the lady in red sitting at the table with a red rose in the vase."

Once your husband arrives and finds his "admirer," the two of you can "get to know each other." Maybe, if you hit it off, you can go back to "her place" for dessert. This is fun and definitely gets romantic results.

—DINA KOEHLY

*D*iscover the answers to these questions. Be open and accepting. You'll be surprised what your husband will share when he feels safe and respected.

- What is the most joyful thing you've experienced?
- What was your hardest experience?
- What are your secret ambitions?
- Who are the five people you most admire and why?
- What are your spiritual struggles?
- What is your favorite piece of my lingerie?
- As a child, what did you dream of doing someday?
- What is your earliest memory?
- What would you consider a sexual treat?

Cell phones can be a wonderful romance tool. My husband and I both have cell phones that are on the same pricing plan so we have free minutes to each other all the time. My husband has a one-hour drive home from work. Every afternoon when he gets off work I call him and begin our playful game of phone tag. During our many phone calls, I might tell him how much I've missed him, or what we're having for dinner, or even how much I'd like to kiss him. We make wise use of that one-hour drive home and turn it into flirt sessions that start the flames of romance before he gets home.

—KIMBERLY OWENS

Rent several of your husband's favorite movies—the ones you normally don't want to see. Watch them with him while you snuggle and feed him popcorn.

—BETH GODDARD

○ ○ ○

Romance turns the kitchen into a fun parlor,
the dining room into a rendezvous,
the bedroom into an island paradise.

R.N. HAWKINS

○ ○ ○

*D*are to befriend your husband. Get into his space and find out what he loves. Be willing to be his prayer partner and his confidant. There is an unbelievable spiritual bond that is possible between you and your man when you agree to get totally clean with God, totally clean with each other, and view each other as intimate friends.

As your husband's confidant, agree to keep his secrets and not get angry if he confesses an area where he's struggling. Have your husband pledge to do the same for you. Pray together as friends and lovers.

The romance in your marriage will heat up!

I've always decorated our home to suit my tastes, but I decided to surprise my guy and create a bedroom he'd appreciate.

After he went to work, I decorated the room to resemble a cozy cabin. I hung framed outdoorsy prints. I placed his gun cabinet along one of the walls, and put an oil lamp on top of it. I hung an old mirror and brought in an antique chest of drawers. Soon I'm going to add a faux fireplace.

I placed a bamboo runner across the top of our dresser and added stacked books and an oil lamp. I put a live ficus tree in one corner. I also used antique lamps on our bedside tables. In the bathroom, I used antique mason jars for mouthwash, cotton balls, and toothpaste. I used an old quilt for a shower curtain, and hung a deer picture.

The bedroom is now our special retreat.

—KIMBERLY OWENS

One evening, I decided to create a romantic atmosphere in the bedroom. While my husband was in the shower, I slipped on a new, slinky, black ooh-la-la, folded the covers down to the foot of the bed, lit a candle, and sprayed perfume on the sheets. As a final touch, I clicked on the bedside radio for some soft background music. Soon I discovered the radio was set on a gospel station. Before I had time to change it, my husband walked into the bedroom. A deep bass voice from the radio belted out the old gospel song, "How long has it been?"

—KRISTY DYKES

How Do I Love Thee

How do I love thee? Let me count the ways.
I love thee to the depth and
breadth and height
my soul can reach, when feeling out of sight
for the ends of Being and ideal Grace.
I love thee to the level of every day's
most quiet need, by sun and candle-light.
I love thee freely, as men strive for right;
I love thee purely, as they turn from praise.
I love thee with the passion put to use
in my old griefs, and with
my childhood's faith.
I love thee with a love I seemed to lose
with my lost saints—I love thee
with the breath,
smiles, tears, of all my life!—
and, if God choose,
I shall but love thee better after death.

ELIZABETH BARRETT BROWNING

I keep romance burning in my marriage by occasionally *not* wearing makeup or fixing my hair. Each time I sport the natural look, I nearly have to arm myself with a wooden spoon to ward off my husband, "Mr. Octopus Hands."

For years I believed my dear husband found me gorgeous and irresistible in my natural glory. But one time I pushed him away and asked why he seemed to be all hands and fingers when I was at my worst. He stood to his full height, and his lips formed a slow smile. "I don't have to worry about messing you up," he said. "You already are."

—JENNIFER JOHNSON

Boast about yourself to your man. Your husband will enjoy hearing you speak sensually of yourself. Tease him with why he should be romantically interested in you. Solomon's lover speaks of her beauty, chastity, breasts, and his contentment with her. She is aware of her imperfections and that others are prettier, but that doesn't stop her from having confidence in the romance she offers him.

The idea of monogamy creates romantic excitement. It excites your spouse to remember that your body is all his…and only his! Remind your spouse of your permanent devotion to him and watch the romance ignite!

—Philip Attebery

When you're mad at your husband, go into the kitchen and bake his favorite dessert. Acting out love enables you to more easily forgive. And it will blow your husband away!

—CHRIS SANDERS

I surprised my husband by renting the honeymoon suite at a local hotel. I had the staff put candles and chilled fruit juice with wine glasses in the bathroom. I lured my husband to the hotel. I hurried into the bathroom, ran a tub of bubbles, climbed in, and called him. But he'd turned on TV and was watching football.

I called him again.

He came into the bathroom and blankly looked at me, his mind on football. "What?"

For a second I decided romance was dead, but I wasn't going to lose the moment. Instead of getting angry, I propped one bare heel on the edge of the tub, held up my glass of juice, and asked, "What do you think?"

His eyebrows rose and he said, "I'll be back." He turned off the TV and joined me.

I tease him about it now, and he says, "But, honey, it was the Broncos!"

—KIM SAWYER

SOFTLY I DANCE
WITH YOU

Softly, softly I dance with you.
Your strong arms hold me
with a tenderness that makes my heart sigh.
We move together
without thought…as one.
Inside my soul whispers,
"How? Tell me why?"

Softly, softly I dance with you
our hearts closely pressed…
touching…beating…
without words whispering love.
For moments in the crowd we are alone,
and find love renewed.
Too soon, oh too soon, our solitude is over.
The world presses upon us, forcing us apart.
So whenever I can…however I may…
softly, softly I'll dance with you,
and only you.

DOROTHY CLARK

My love came near me,
and with arms even then so strong and true,
held me close to his faithful heart,
whispering words of comfort and hope.
His kisses still enraptured me,
and his embrace brought waves of desire.
Never will cold or want or age,
diminish the joy of our bond.

ROBERT OSBORNE

PART TWO

Making Your Lady Swoon

A woman wants a man she can look up to who won't look down on her.
Stan Toler

I wanted to surprise my husband with a gift certificate to a local golf course and tell him he was meeting a friend there at a certain time. I deliberated which friend I should invite. Finally, after a lot of thinking, I decided to tell him about my plan and ask him what friend he wanted to invite.

He thought for a few seconds and then smiled. "I want *you* to go with me," he said.

I glowed with pleasure because I never imagined he'd choose me. So I went golfing with him. We spent several hours together on the golf course and had a blast!

This was one of the best gifts my husband has ever given me. I felt so honored and adored to know that he'd choose me over all his male friends.

*T*he home is an extension of most wives' hearts. Ask your wife for a "honey-do" list. If there's any way you can perform the chores, do them for her whether you hate them or not.

∘ ∘ ∘

WHAT DOES LOVE MEAN?

Four- to eight-year-olds were asked, "What does love mean?" Enjoy their replies!

"When my grandmother got arthritis, she couldn't bend over and paint her toenails anymore. So my grandfather does it for her all the time, even when his hands got arthritis, too. That's love." (REBECCA—AGE 8)

"When someone loves you, the way they say your name is different. You know your name is safe in their mouth." (BILLY—AGE 4)

○ ○

"Love is when you go out to eat and give somebody most of your French fries without making them give you any of theirs." (CHRISSY—AGE 6)

"Love is what makes you smile when you're tired." (TERRI—AGE 4)

"Love is when my mommy makes coffee for my daddy, and she takes a sip before giving it to him to make sure the taste is okay." (DANNY—AGE 7)

"Love is what's in the room with you at Christmas if you stop opening presents and listen." (BOBBY—AGE 5)

"Love is when you tell a guy you like his shirt, and then he wears it every day." (NOELLE—AGE 7)

"When you love somebody, your eyelashes go up and down and little stars come out of you." (KAREN—AGE 7)

"You really shouldn't say 'I love you' unless you mean it. But if you mean it, you should say it a lot. People forget." (JESSICA—AGE 8)

*A*sk your wife to tell you what her most hated household chore is, and then promise to faithfully perform that chore for one year. After that year, ask her if she'd like you to add another chore to your list or switch the first chore with another one. Then commit to another year of serving her in this fashion. Annually evaluate your commitment.

I value my wife's contribution to our family. I hug her often and encourage her in her writing and speaking ministry. When I recognize that her spirits are low, I try to lift her up. The way I see it, romance sometimes involves the intangible such as verbal encouragement, listening, and reaching that inner person only I know.

—PAUL NIXON

Regularly take the time to be still and listen to your wife. Look into her eyes, stroke her face, hold her hand, ask nothing in return. Simply let her know that every word she says is of monumental importance to you.

Commit 30 minutes a day to simply listening to your wife and valuing her enough to focus solely upon her. Even if what she wants to talk about really doesn't concern you, listen. She will feel like a treasured queen, and her adoration for you will increase.

—WANDA BRUNSTETTER

o o o

Many waters cannot quench love;
rivers cannot wash it away.
If one were to give
all the wealth of his house for love,
it would be utterly scorned.

SONG OF SONGS 8:7

*A*rrange to take a day off and declare it a special holiday for your wife. If you have kids, make arrangements for their care. If your wife has a career, secretly arrange with her boss for her to take the day off. That morning tell her you're her "knight in shining armor," awaiting her beck and call. Then do whatever she wants the whole day.

Depending on your wife's interests and tastes, you might end up shopping, checking into a hotel with a Jacuzzi and spending the day lazing around, going to garage sales, painting her toenails, swimming, hiking, or golfing. Whatever you plan, make certain it's something *she* genuinely enjoys.

On your anniversary buy a flower for every *month* you've been married, rather than every year. If you've been married more than a year or two, this bouquet will be *huge*. That's the whole point! To keep this economical, scout out discount department stores that sell fresh flowers. You can buy bouquets of 20 to 30 mixed flowers for a few dollars.

My husband made a certificate on the computer that said, "This love certificate entitles Sophie to a full body massage at the time of her choosing. This coupon is valid for one year. Be sure to ask about our 1,000 kisses promotion."

—SOPHIE LAURIE

○ ○ ○

Within the heart of every woman
lies the desire to be loved
by a man who will
surrender his life for her.

ERIC WIGGIN

○ ○ ○

*W*rite a love note to your wife "just because." List all the reasons you think she's beautiful. Include several traits from her personality, her spirituality, and her physical attributes.

My husband jogs almost every day. When he returns, he always has a miniature bouquet of wildflowers in his hand. He finds these growing in an open field by our house and picks one or two. Sometimes they're just weeds that have bloomed, but they're still quite intricate and beautiful. After picking them, he jogs the rest of the way home, carrying the flowers in his hand. When he walks through the door, he hands them to me. "They're from God's garden," he says. I place them by my computer keyboard and enjoy them the rest of the day.

—MARTHA BOLTON

*W*anting to see the display of meteors that would be in the sky for a few nights, my husband drove us out to the country, where there were no city lights and nothing but black, inky night full of twinkling lights and meteors streaking across the sky. As we sat on the hood of the car and watched the magical scene, I kept thinking, *Now this is romantic.*

—WANDA BRUNSTETTER

*A*fter dinner give your wife the evening off. Insist on doing the dishes. And after the kitchen is clean, spoil her with a lavish foot massage and ask nothing in return. If you really want to astound her, repeat this for one week.

*I*nvite your wife on a red (or other color) date. Incorporate the color throughout your time together. Here are some ideas…

- Ask her to wear her favorite color.
- Wear a tie or suit or shirt in that color.
- Make reservations at a restaurant and request a tablecloth in her favorite color.
- Present her with a bouquet of flowers in her color.
- Arrange for as much food as you can from that color group.
- Buy your wife real or costume jewelry with a stone in her color.
- Get your mate a new T-shirt, or hiking shorts, or whatever in her color.
- Give her lingerie in her special color. She might treat you to a style show!

Romance is an attitude, a state of mind. It comes from within. You only have to look for it and develop it. Don't keep wishing you or your husband were more romantic. Do something about it. If you have an image in your mind of what romance is, make the image come to life. Dress the part. Perform the actions. Purchase whatever is necessary. Most importantly, stop preparing to live and start living.

AMBER MILLER

*M*y man and two kids wowed me. The kids made a fruit tray garnished with cheese and crackers. My husband scattered candles around the bathroom. He drew a hot bath and put the fruit tray and my favorite books on the commode lid. The kids scattered rose petals from the front door to the bathroom and taped an invitation to relax on the door.

When I arrived, I read the note and followed the rose-petal trail. Opening the bathroom door I saw lit candles, a steaming bath, fluffy towels, my robe, a wonderful snack, and iced tea in a crystal goblet!

I heard giggles behind my bedroom door. I gave everyone hugs and disappeared into my private spa.

Wow! My son saw how to do something special for a wife; my daughter learned what wonderful husbands do. And my honey held a ready-for-lovin' wife that night!

—LYNETTE SOWELL

 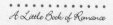

On New Year's Eve or July 4th, buy a special round of fireworks just for your wife. Before setting them off, tell her she's about to get an example of how she affects you. Then light the fireworks and watch her eyes sparkle.

For our last wedding anniversary, my husband surprised me with a trip to Boston and New York. He sent me a cute e-mail card in which he told me that we would be taking a trip and the dates we would be going—one word on one line at a time. At the bottom of his message he included websites for me to discover each place we were to visit, each hotel, and the Broadway plays. I felt like a kid in a candy store!

—DiAnn Mills

Take a couple of weeks to discreetly learn what your wife's favorite breakfast includes. After she's asleep one Friday night, sneak out to an all-night grocery store and buy every item on her list. Surprise her the next morning with breakfast in bed.

Solomon calls his lover a "lily among thorns" (Song of Songs 2:2). He speaks intimately of her and describes her cheeks, neck, eyes, temples, hair, teeth, lips, mouth, breasts, feet, thighs, waist, nose, head, figure, and breath. He also compliments her attire and perfume.

What lady would not be encouraged by a husband's flattery of her entire anatomy and her taste in what she wears? A wife can be primed toward romance by consistent and ongoing verbal admiration from her husband!

—PHILIP ATTEBERY

 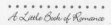

○ ○

○ ○ ○

Love is patient, love is kind.
It does not envy, it does not boast,
it is not proud. It is not rude,
it is not self-seeking,
it is not easily angered,
it keeps no record of wrongs.
Love does not delight in evil but
rejoices with the truth.
It always protects, always trusts,
always hopes,
always perseveres.
Love never fails....

1 CORINTHIANS 13:4-8

○ ○ ○

*O*n my birthday, even though I knew we would probably do something that evening, I felt a big letdown when my husband left for work and the kids went to school. Was I ever surprised when soon after the children departed, Richard showed up at the back door. As a special birthday present, he'd taken the day off work. We went shopping, out to lunch, and had several romantic hours alone.

—WANDA BRUNSTETTER

My husband loves to give me surprises. It doesn't have to be a special occasion for him to suddenly announce, "You have one hour to pack for a ____-day trip. These are the kind of clothes you will need." He always has the smallest detail worked out.

—DiAnn Mills

I cut out 30 small white strips of paper and wrote on each of them romantic things I would do for my wife. I put them into a pill bottle. I created a prescription label and taped it on the outside of the bottle with directions for her to take out a piece of paper each day. Some of the items were "honey dos" and others involved dinner out at her favorite dining place or something as simple as a free back rub. What a month of fun!

—STAN TOLER

Because I get up earlier in the mornings than my husband to work out, he always makes the bed, brews the coffee, and has the newspaper ready for us to read together when I get home. I love it!

—DiAnn Mills

*W*hat unique ways can express your excitement for your wife and the pleasures of romance in your marriage? How can you illustrate to her that she is your choice out of all the women in the world? Solomon used creative and sensual illustrations to describe his romantic feelings toward his lover.

Sixty queens there may be,
and eighty concubines,
and virgins beyond numbers;
but my dove, my perfect one, is unique...

SONG OF SONGS 6:8

Solomon gets steamy by describing his lover's breasts as clusters of fruit in a palm tree. He says, "I will climb the palm tree, I will take hold of its fruit!"

—PHILIP ATTEBERY

*F*or Valentine's Day last year, I sent my wife a dozen roses and went shopping at Victoria's Secret for her. I purchased sleepwear as well as some of her favorite lotions and had them gift wrapped. I packed her luggage and picked her up at work. I then drove her to the nicest Marriott in our town. We stayed Friday and Saturday night.

—STAN TOLER

At a speaking engagement where I was the keynote speaker and particularly nervous, my husband sent flowers 30 minutes before my talk. It eased my nerves and his sweet words on the card made me love him even more.

—DiAnn Mills

∘ ∘ ∘

Knight in Shining Armor

Strong, gentle, caring, loving you.
You are my knight in shining armor,
though sometimes the shine is hard to see
when daily hassles cloud the view.
But you're always there—
steady, quiet, and sure.
What would I do without you—
my anchor, my playmate, my lover.
How empty my life would be
without strong, gentle, caring, loving you!

DEBRA WHITE SMITH

*N*eeding to get away by ourselves but too poor to stay at a hotel, my husband gathered up our old tent, sleeping bags, and camping gear, and off we went to the woods. What could be more romantic than sitting around the campfire, roasting marshmallows, and listening to my husband play his harmonica and sing?

—WANDA BRUNSTETTER

My best birthday present is butcher paper! My husband started a creative 8-foot banner tradition and then got the kids involved. They dream up the slogan weeks in advance. The day before or the day of my birthday they get me out of the house and get to work. The banners feature colorful, two-foot-high letters proclaiming:

> 33 and Full of Glee
> 34 with Looks Galore
> 50 and She's Real Nifty
> 60 and Cute as a Pixie

Here are anniversary banner suggestions:

> 2 and We Still Coo
> 5 and Our Love Thrives
> 6 and We Still Click
> 10 and I'd Marry You Again

—JILL ELIZABETH NELSON

*B*e willing to pray with your wife. Many wives long for their husbands to share prayer and Bible reading with them. As my husband and I grow in this joint endeavor, I am amazed at how this spiritual pursuit bonds us as nothing else does. It's very encouraging for me to hear my husband pray for me; he likewise finds peace and comfort in my praying for him.

When we ask God's blessing upon our union, we carry with us an inner sense that the force who created us is anointing our endeavors. Whether your marriage is on the rocks or thriving, committing to regularly praying together will add a power and strength to your marriage you never imagined.

My husband and I have been married almost 35 years, and I must confess that he is the romantic. Since the first years of our marriage he has made a habit of leaving me the letters ILY ("I Love You") in different places around the house and in various mediums. The first one I can remember was made out of huge strips of toilet paper on our kitchen floor. He has also spelled it out on the kitchen table with candy and toothpicks. One time he tore the letters out of pieces of paper and put them in a letter and mailed them to me. We often leave little notes for each other on the kitchen table or front door and sign them ILY.

—Rose Allen McCauley

A PRACTICAL LOVE

My husband is a mechanical genius, but
he doesn't consider himself a home-
improvement guru. Nevertheless, when
I explained to him that I was on the
verge of hyperventilating over how bad
our house was looking, he immediately
rolled up his sleeves and went to work.

After struggling for a whole Saturday to pull
up our bathroom tile, he looked at me and
said, "I hate doing this. I hate it! The only
reason I'm doing it is because I love you!"
The honest frustration on his face mingling
with the love in his eyes was as beautiful
as any bouquet of roses he's ever offered.

DEBRA WHITE SMITH

*B*uy your wife a rosebush. When the bush blooms, fix her a bouquet. Tell her you'll take care of the bush as a labor of love for her. When you fertilize and water, she'll be reminded of your love.

When choosing a bush, consider color:

Red: Love, beauty, courage, and respect

White: Purity, innocence, humility

Pink: Appreciation, happiness, admiration

Dark pink: Appreciation, gratitude

Light pink: Admiration, sympathy

Orange: Desire and enthusiasm

Red and white: Together they signify unity

Red rosebud: Purity and loveliness

White rosebud: Girlhood

Thornless rose: "Love at first sight"

*W*omen are like fine automobiles that need to sit and purr a while before driving. Any good mechanic knows you get the best performance out of a vehicle if you treat it with tender loving care. The same holds true for women and sex.

Mark one day a week as "Project Seduction." Start that morning with a phone call from work, telling your wife she's the most spectacular woman alive. An hour or so later e-mail her a compliment. Mid-morning ask her to lunch. During lunch whisper in her ear how she turns you on. Mid-afternoon call and offer a few details of how you're planning to make love to her.

Also do this on trips. If you and your wife are driving somewhere, don't waste the time with chitchat. Begin with a few sincere compliments that grow into talking seductively. If you invest time into talking sexy to your wife, you'll be surprised at how revved her engine will become.

Take your wife golfing or fishing or hunting or whatever your hobby involves. Arrange for a bouquet of flowers or special gift to be placed at a strategic place—for instance, in your tackle box or your golf bag. Then ask her for something from the exact spot where you've placed the gift so she'll find it and be surprised.

○ ○ ○

RABBI BEN EZRA

Grow old along with me!
The best is yet to be,
the last of life, for which the first was made:
our times are in His hand
who saith "A whole I planned,
youth shows but half; trust God:
see all nor be afraid!"

ROBERT BROWNING

On the snow-covered hillside outside our kitchen window my husband stamped out a 50-foot heart with the letters C+R in the middle. I didn't notice it, so he suggested we take a walk. A neighbor asked if we'd noticed someone making tracks in our field. He thought it was someone's initials. That's when I finally realized what my husband had done!

The next year I stuck glow-in-the-dark stars on our bedroom ceiling in the shape of a heart with ILY (I love you) in the center. But he was not to be outdone! He climbed onto our barn roof and painted a big red heart with C+R in it. It's still there and so is the heart of stars on our bedroom ceiling. Whoever said "love is for the young" didn't know my husband—still my knight in shining armor after 35 years!

—Rose Allen McCauley

*I*magine your wife is the lover you always dreamed of having in your life. If she *were* that lover, how would you treat her? You would *ask her* what she dreams of in a lover, and do everything in your power to live that. Life is too short to not take advantage of every opportunity!

Don't become so obsessed with your work, your bills, your car, your home, that you neglect the most important relationship in your life—the one with your wife. Cultivate the relationship. Pursue your wife as you did before you were married. Before you know it, your wife will become your dream lover.

—AMBER MILLER

I chase dreams like a child chases summer butterflies. My husband chooses presents accordingly. For example, early in my marriage I had a passion for volleyball. Despite the fact that I spent many evenings away, my husband bought me a leather volleyball as a nod of acceptance that said, "You're free to chase the butterfly."

He seemed amused when I focused on cartooning. I checked out how-to books and practiced. Seeing my determination, my husband bought me an art kit, paintbrushes, and paper. His gift lifted my spirit, saying, "That butterfly you're chasing looks pretty lofty. Here's a butterfly net to help you reach higher." I didn't become a cartoonist, but I did design a school mascot and win first place in an amateur art contest.

When I decided to learn Spanish, my husband loaned me his old Spanish books from high school. He corrected my horrid pronunciations patiently. I glowed when he told his friends I taught myself Spanish.

Finally I discovered writing. I realized writing always hovered near my soul, a beautiful butterfly waiting patiently since childhood for me to notice its flight. After I won my first writing contest, I joined a writer's group. My husband gave up some of his evening plans so I could attend meetings. His sacrifice let me know I was free to chase the butterfly. After my first publication, my husband handed me a butterfly net in the form of a notebook and fancy pen.

I treasure my unlikely ensemble of gifts: a ball, paintbrushes, a smile, and pens. My husband has taught me what it means to romance someone. The actions, attitudes, and words you gift your spouse with demonstrate your belief in him or her. When your mate chases butterflies, it is your privilege to be the gentle wind whispering, "Your dreams are important. Follow your heart. I'm right behind you."

—LORI Z. SCOTT

My husband turned our loft into a beautiful garden using plants from all over the house, soft lights, music, and chilled juice. There we had our own romantic picnic—all without leaving the house.

—REBECCA BARLOW JORDAN

PART THREE

The Hero and the Lady

*There are three things that are too
amazing for me,
four that I do not understand:
the way of an eagle in the sky,
the way of a snake on a rock,
the way of a ship on the high seas,
and the way of a man with a maiden.*

Proverbs 30:18-19

With three teenagers in the home wise to every move we made, it was hard for my husband and me to find any time to talk together. It seemed every sentence was interrupted or commented upon by the kids, even if what we were talking about had nothing to do with them. Even an innocent kiss on the cheek received whistles, jeers, or "I know what you two are going to be doing!" Short of triple homicide, we devised a clever plan for privacy.

After dinner we took our coffee cups and wandered out to the car, rolled up all the windows and locked the doors. We warned the children not to come out unless somebody was seriously injured. Those few moments alone in the car, sipping coffee and talking about whatever we wanted, were like dewdrops on a thirsty tongue.

—LINDA RONDEAU

Kick your way through fallen leaves. Gather them into a pile and jump or fall into them together. Repeat.

—AMBER MILLER

○ ○

SEDUCTION

The act was deliberate,
slow…focused….
Reaching across
barriers…distances.
The move was secretive,
enticing…stimulating.
It was well-rehearsed
yet spontaneous,
seducing…capturing.

The desire was whispering,
waiting…longing…
linking lovers intimately
with…
a wink!

R.N. HAWKINS **and**
DEBRA WHITE SMITH

Reluctant at first, my husband finally agreed to join me for an early morning pedicure at my favorite nail salon. The soon-as-the-doors-opened appointment ensured the privacy I perceived his ego needed. He was so amazed at how rejuvenated his feet and legs felt he suggested we go for a walk along the nature trail in a nearby state park. Already in warm-ups and tennis shoes, we stopped for bottled water and a trail-mix snack. Later we shared this "lunch" atop the most beautiful peak in the park. Walking for his diabetes and our health now includes an occasional pedicure and a special getaway for just the two of us.

—LIN HARRIS

We made a commitment years ago to keep one weeknight open. That is our date night. If it is not an emergency, we don't let anything interfere with our special time. We do different things such as go out for coffee or a movie, or we just have a quiet evening at home with romantic music, candlelight, and conversation.

—SUSAN NEUFELD

Last June I went on one of my husband's business trips with him. We drove to Denver, stopped for dinner in Loveland, Colorado, on our way in, and then went to the Walmart Supercenter. We looked at our watches and gave ourselves 30 minutes to each go our separate ways in the store and buy some things to make the evenings special. We had so much fun! We bumped into each other a couple of times and both of us quickly tried to hide what we were going to purchase. As the next two days unfolded we set times to break out the items we had bought. It really was a lot of fun.

—KIM MASKELL

*I*f you've been married a while, buy an "oldies" CD that features popular love songs from when you were dating. Spend an evening listening and swaying to the music. As you share memories from those years when you were first falling in love, you'll be surprised at how new your love will feel.

For many years, we have followed the advice of pastor/evangelist Paul Burleson, who says to "Divert Daily," "Withdraw Weekly," and "Abandon Annually." My husband and I find ourselves more and more loving to "Abandon Quarterly" to a nice hotel or wonderful bed-and-breakfast. We've made lots of fantastic memories, and it keeps our marriage fresh with anticipation and romantic enjoyment. We started doing this when our children were small—and I am now a grandmother.

—REBECCA BARLOW JORDAN

My wife and I have a lot of fun shopping for "romantic intentions." We check into a hotel and then look for places to shop. (We don't have to leave town, but going away means more freedom for romance.) The trip isn't for buying so much as it's for enjoying each other in romantic attire.

Let your spouse decide what he or she wants you to try on. Remove limits of styles, colors, and price. Let your spouse see you in things you don't normally wear. It might spark passion! Maybe he wants to see you in evening wear. Maybe she yearns to see you in tighter jeans. Enjoy each other!

Create a budget, including how much to spend on clothes. Give each other ideas on the clothes you may ask the other to try on by showing pictures from catalogs or pointing out items in stores.

—PHILIP ATTEBERY

 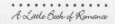

My marriage has benefited from an online affair. My husband frequently has job assignments that keep him away for months at a time, with only weekend visits home. During those periods when he is away, we have an online affair *with each other* to keep romance alive. We flirt online and look forward to the weekends he is home.

—CANDY ARRINGTON

My husband and I exchange heart gifts and cards. Once a year we like to get creative and artistic with these homemade cards. On the inside we write three things we really appreciate about our mate. These are usually character qualities our partner has shown over the past year or areas of growth we've noticed. Then we each give one gift from our heart. It is usually a promise to do something special for our partner during the next year. It can be something like praying daily for him or her, beginning a weekly date night, focusing on appreciation of the spouse, or helping with a particular need. Heart gifts help keep the romance alive in our marriage.

—CARRIE TURANSKY

Create an inexpensive adventure date. Go to the train station or bus station and catch the first ride to wherever it's going. Explore the area together and learn something new. No matter where it is, you'll be seeing it together. You'll find something there for just the two of you, and it will make the journey special.

—AMBER MILLER

THE UNSPOKEN

I was…
attracted by your walk, arrested by your grace,
accepted by your look, aroused by your touch.
The pleasure of the unspoken.

I was…
beguiled by a smile, bewitched by a wink,
bothered by a frown, broken by a tear.
The power of the unspoken.

I was…
charmed by your style, captivated by your sparkle,
comforted by your spirit, consumed by your love.
The wonder of the unspoken.

R.N. HAWKINS

Sharing your partner's dreams and goals really helps you connect on a heart level. Why not plan a special night out and prepare several questions that relate to goals and dreams. Ask your mate, "What would you like to do as a job or ministry if money were not an issue?" or "What do you see yourself doing in five years?" or "What vacation would you take if you could go anywhere in the world?" These are fun questions that will give you insights into your mate's dreams and desires. Then consider how you can encourage your partner to reach some of those goals.

—CARRIE TURANSKY

*M*y husband was in the Air Force and was sent to Thailand twice. One of the ways we romanced each other during those times was writing letters almost every day. Something else we did every day was read our Bibles and pray at the same time, allowing for the 12-hour time difference. I copied a list of New Testament readings, and we both read through the whole New Testament the first year he was away, reading the same selection at the same time. Even though we were separated by 12,000 miles, we were joined spiritually.

A speaker once gave an illustration I've never forgotten. He said marriage is like a triangle with God at the apex and each spouse at the two points of the base. As we each grow closer to God, the base moves upward and we grow closer to one another.

—ROSE ALLEN McCAULEY

My wife and I have a standing lunch date once a week. It doesn't matter what day of the week or which restaurant we choose, as long as we get away by ourselves. Sometimes we have a picnic in the city park or drive to a hilltop lookout for a scenic getaway.

—RONNIE JOHNSON

Combine romance with a little house-work. During the day take a couple of hours to clean your car, collecting all the spare change you find under the seats and between the cracks. Do the same inside your house with the couches and chairs. Clean them and collect the loose change.

Combine all the change you find, along with the money in your wallets and pockets, and make an evening out of it. It might only be enough to split an ice-cream sundae at a local fast-food restaurant. Or you might be surprised and find enough for some fine dining and even a rented movie afterward. Be creative with your use of the buried trea-sure you've uncovered.

—CHRISTY BARRITT

We rose up,
canceled weekend business,
left the house a mess.
Picnic on the beach.
Lips within reach.
Love refreshed,
heart in heart.

We worshiped God today
as the three of us played.

R.N. AND MARY HAWKINS

I leave unexpected gifts on my wife's desk at work when she is elsewhere. She really loves it when I surprise her with flowers. A gift on her birthday and our anniversary is expected, so I choose to celebrate this way on days when she doesn't expect it. Every time someone comments on the flowers, it reminds her that I want everyone to know we are in love.

—RONNIE JOHNSON

*C*arve out some couple time, even if the getaway doesn't seem like a date. My husband and I are members of a county Political Executive Committee; we know one evening every month we will be working together as a couple for causes and issues we believe in and support. My husband was on the committee first and recruited me. One of the reasons I joined was because it gave me the opportunity to work with my husband. This togetherness has strengthened our marriage because it refocuses us as a team.

—JANET KAWASH

*P*oetry is a major part of the romantic journey my husband and I share, especially the poetry of Elizabeth and Robert Browning. Poetry fuels our romance.

We framed our silhouettes done at Montmartre Art Colony in Paris as a reminder of our love. In the center, in calligraphy, is Elizabeth Barrett Browning's "How do I love thee?" When our parents died and mortality sank in, Robert Browning's "Grow old along with me, the best is yet to be" became our mantra.

One Christmas I tracked down an antique, leather-bound copy of the works of Robert and Elizabeth Browning for my husband. While clearing the gift-opening chaos, I looked up to see him rub his hand softly across the cover. His face glowed with appreciation. Love poems are a tradition that helps keep the spark of romance fresh.

—JUDYTHE HIXSON

*L*et everyone know you love someone! My wife's desk is next to the check-out counter in the front of a library, and she displays candid snapshots of me in sight of students checking out books. When a new student sees a picture of me showing off a large bass or posing on vacation, he often figures out my wife and I are married. It makes me feel good to know she wants everyone to know we are together.

—RONNIE JOHNSON

○ ○

○ ○ ○

Sometimes in our earnestness
to do life right,
we forget to play!
When was the last time you
and your love played?
If you can't remember,
well…it's playtime!

DOLLEY CARLSON
Mr. and Mrs. Gifts from the Heart

○ ○ ○

One time we went to the hospital to call on a woman in our church. We had just stepped onto the elevator. Nobody else was in there with us, and Richard pulled me into his arms, gazed lovingly into my eyes, and said, "Have I told you lately how much I love and appreciate you?"

—WANDA BRUNSTETTER

*D*uring our many years together, my husband and I have kept our love alive. As I examine each "heart moment" a smile curves my lips. Some memories make me blush: My seductive whisper promising an intimate evening inadvertently broadcast via my husband's speaker phone to an office filled with executives. The e-mail about his sexy fragrance lingering in our room that received the "hot pepper" warning flag from the company firewall for explicit content.

Memories of bed-and-breakfast weekends and hand-in-hand walks through Butchart Gardens in Victoria, Canada, a field of heather in Scotland, the streets of New York, and our neighborhood link us.

Institute a special "remembering date." Focus on the wonderful times you've enjoyed as a couple. And don't forget the funny moments.

—Judythe Hixson

Since my husband and I can't afford to go out to dinner, pay for a babysitter, and the like, our alone time comes in very simple ways. Every Sunday when the kids go outside to play or are otherwise occupied, my husband and I sit down together and do the Sunday crossword. Ever since we started dating, the Sunday crossword has been a ritual we *always* do together. And our vocabulary has increased twofold.

—TRACY FARNSWORTH

One year my husband and I had very little money to celebrate our anniversary, so I dropped off our two children at my parents' place, came home, fixed us a candlelight dinner, and then got dressed in my prettiest dress. After dinner my husband and I built a fire in the fireplace, hauled our mattress off the bed, and slept in front of the glowing embers. It was one of the most memorable anniversaries we've ever had.

—WANDA BRUNSTETTER

*A*fter the kids go to bed and the house gets quiet, I run a bubble bath in our garden tub and light several candles. My husband and I turn off the lights, sit in the tub in the candlelight, and enjoy the silence and each other. It is a very relaxing and romantic way to end our day.

—KIM DAVIS

YOU ARE BEAUTIFUL, MY LOVE

You are beautiful, my love.
You have a beauty the years cannot take away...
a beauty enhanced by the
laughter lines around your eyes,
the tinges of gray in your hair.

The source of your beauty is not found in cosmetics.
Your beauty comes from within.
Your spirit rejoices in God's grace
and seeps to the surface.
Joy, shining through sparkling eyes,
flashing smile, caring fingers....

You are beautiful, my love.
I thank God continually for you.
I thank Him for His mercy in allowing me to
drink of your beauty all these years.
What a joy it is to know that I will behold
your redeemed beauty,
in His presence, eternally.
Praise His wonderful name!

R.N. HAWKINS

THE PHENOMENAL
FREEDOM TO LOVE

Understanding that God gave you unique
gifts and gave your wife unique gifts frees
you to accept your mate exactly the way
she is. Every man doesn't possess the same
set of gifts; neither does every woman. We
are individuals created by God. Once you
realize these truths, you will stop expect-
ing your partner to manifest her gifts and
yours too. You will fully understand that the
two of you are equal halves of a whole. You
are indeed a team! And you will discover a
phenomenal freedom to unconditionally love
and accept your mate as you see yourself
as her playmate, her lover, her husband.

ABOUT THE AUTHOR

Debra White Smith continues to impact and entertain readers with her life-changing books, including *Romancing Your Husband, Romancing Your Wife,* The Sisters Suspense series, The Austen series, and The Debutantes series. She's an award-winning author, including such honors as Top-10 Reader Favorite, Gold Medallion finalist, and Retailer's Choice Award finalist. Debra has more than 50 books to her credit and over a million books in print.

The founder of Real Life Ministries, Debra recently launched Real Life Minute, which airs on radio stations nationwide. She also speaks passionately with insight and humor at ministry events across the nation. Debra has been featured on a variety of media, including *The 700 Club, At Home Life, Getting Together, Moody Broadcasting Network, Fox News, Viewpoint,* and *America's Family Coaches.* She holds an M.A. in English.

Debra lives in small-town America with her husband, two children, and a herd of cats.

To write Debra or contact her for speaking engagements, check out her website:

www.debrawhitesmith.com

or send mail to

Real Life Ministries
Daniel W. Smith, Ministry Manager
PO Box 1482,
Jacksonville, TX 75766

or call

1-866-211-3400

Romancing Your Husband
by Debra White Smith

Early days in a relationship are exhilarating, but they can't touch the thrilling love affair you can have now. Cutting through traditional misconceptions and exploring every facet of the Bible's message on marriage, *Romancing Your Husband* reveals how you can create a union others only dream about.

From making Jesus an active part of your marriage to arranging fantastic romantic interludes, you'll discover how to—

- make romance a reality
- "knock your husband's socks off"
- become a lover-wife, not a mother-wife
- find freedom in forgiving
- cultivate a sacred romance with God

Experience fulfillment through romancing your husband...and don't be surprised when he romances you back!

Romancing Your Wife

by Debra White Smith and Daniel W. Smith

Do you want your husband to surprise you and put more romance in your relationship? *Romancing Your Wife* can help! Give this book to your hubby, and he'll discover ways to create an exciting, enthusiastic marriage.

Debra and her husband, Daniel, offer biblical wisdom and practical advice that when put into practice will help your husband mentally, emotionally, and physically improve his relationship with you. He'll discover tools to build a dynamite marriage, including how to—

- communicate his love more effectively
- make you feel cherished
- better understand your needs and wants
- create a unity of spirit and mind
- increase the passion in your marriage

From insights on little things that jazz up a marriage to more than 20 "Endearing Encounters," *Romancing Your Wife* sets the stage for love and romance.